Your Child's]

Nurturing healthy self-esteem
and relationships

Dr. Sandra Johnson

Published by S L J Johnson Pty Ltd

Sydney, Australia

National Library of Australia Cataloguing-in-Publication entry:

Author: Johnson, Sandra Lucille, author.
Title: Your child's development: nurturing healthy self-esteem and
    relationships / Dr Sandra Johnson.
Edition: First edition.
ISBN: 9780987548245 (paperback)
Subjects: Child development--Handbooks, manuals, etc.
Dewey Number: 612.65

Cover Design by NatsPearlDesign

Dedication

This book is dedicated to my siblings Elaine, Clarence, Marlene and Arthur who each had a significant influence on my development

Acknowledgements

I am very grateful to friends and colleagues who read and gave comment to this book. I especially want to thank Dr Marlene Johnson for her input as a psychiatrist, and Dr Debbie Perkins for her input as a community child health medical officer.

A special thank you to Victoria Dore who edited the book and to my husband John Lock who edited, formatted and assisted with the publication of this book.

I also want to acknowledge friends, family and colleagues that play such a huge role in my life and for their loving contributions to my personal experiences.

Preface

In my work with families over the past 30 years I have been impressed at the length that parents will go to, in order to help their children. It is with this in mind that I have been inspired to write this book. I do not have all the answers, but I have learned so much from parents and children that I would like to share the insights that I have gained from their experiences through my work as a developmental paediatrician.

'Your Child's Development' is a succinct guide for parents which is practical and easy to follow. It provides busy parents with a ready reference to empower them to raise happy and confident children. The book discusses nurturing the development of your child's self-esteem and relationships with others. It provides a practical approach to child rearing from infancy through to adolescence, and is based on sound psychological and child development principles.

This book is also beneficial to anyone working with children such as teachers, therapists and carers. It aims to enhance positive communication with children and adolescents to foster healthy relationships in the short and long term.

This book is not intended for parents of children with any specific developmental problems. My aim in writing this book is to share thoughts, concepts and ideas that I have gathered from various teachers, writers, colleagues, friends and family. This is an important work because if parents, carers and all persons working with young people have a greater understanding of child development they are more likely to enhance the development of happy, sensitive and thoughtful individuals. This in turn has enormous implications for the future of our society.

My work and training as a paediatrician in Child Development has brought me in contact with children who have a wide range of problems such as learning difficulties, language disorders, attention problems, communication difficulties, autism, developmental disabilities, cerebral palsy and developmental delay. Within my child development practice, which spans 26 years, I have seen many children who do not have any of these specific problems but who instead are dealing with emotional difficulties, adjustment problems, school refusal, bullying and many other issues that children face on a day-to-day basis.

I write this book as an aid for parents and carers in the knowledge that greater understanding fosters tolerance, respect and nurturing for the most vulnerable in our society, our children.

About the author

Dr Sandra L J Johnson. MBChB, DPaed, FRACP, FRCPCH, FACLM.

Dr Sandra Johnson, key author of a book for doctors called 'A Clinical Handbook on Child Development Paediatrics' has written 'Your Child's Development' specifically for parents. Dr Johnson is a developmental paediatrician who, having worked in the field of child development for over 26 years at various international teaching hospitals, draws from a breadth of clinical and teaching experience. She is a clinical senior lecturer at the University of Sydney Medical School in the Discipline of Paediatrics and Child Health. She teaches child development to medical students and postgraduate paediatric trainees.

Table of Contents

Introduction

In order to help our children to develop to the best of their potential we need an understanding of some of the principles of child development. By understanding how relationships evolve, as children move through developmental stages from infancy to adolescence, we appreciate how important relationships affect their self-concept and self-esteem.

This book is not intended to be a detailed text on child development, child psychology or behaviour. The aim is to increase awareness of important factors that promote the development of emotionally healthy and happy children.

The first two chapters deal with the relationships experienced as the child moves from infancy through to adolescence. The focus of these chapters is the developmental process and how relationships change over time.

Chapter 3 focuses on the importance of the preschool years in fostering good relationships with parents and carers. The child's primary relationship is with their parents and this relationship has a powerful influence over future relationships. For the purposes of this book I refer to parents but ask that the reader substitute other primary carers, where relevant, as being persons or individuals who provide the immediate care for the child from infancy through to adolescence.

Chapter 4 focuses on self-esteem and the development of self-concept and chapter 5 addresses the ways that we can promote the development of a healthy self-concept in our children.

Chapter 6 deals with children's behaviour. This chapter discusses the ways that children respond or react when we interact with them, and how we reinforce their behaviour by the way we respond or react to them. Reinforcement of behaviour occurs positively or negatively depending on how we communicate with our children. The importance of boundaries and rules in dealing with children's behaviour is discussed in this chapter.

Chapter 7 discusses how parents encourage their children to have personal responsibility. The important issue of bullying is covered in this chapter.

Chapter 8 focuses on how we communicate with our children. The aim is to raise awareness of the effect that our negative thoughts and negative interactions have on our children. The chapter refers to the issues discussed in chapters 4 and 5 about helping children to develop a healthy self-concept.

Finally, Chapter 9 provides a summary of suggestions to help children develop a healthy self-concept to encourage happy and confident individuals that will contribute to society in adulthood.

1: Experiences and Relationships in Early Childhood

It is well recognised that early experiences impact on the development of a child's self-concept in ways that we cannot easily measure and yet the influence is significant. As infants mature their experiences mould their responses and their interactions with others, and they continually learn about their place in the world and how they can affect others.

Infancy

Babies respond to their environment from the moment of birth and there is evidence to suggest that even while in utero they are sensitive to their environment, particularly to sounds such as their mother's heart beat and even her voice. It not surprising therefore that the mother's mental state, for example anxiety, can have an impact on the baby. Chronic anxiety and stress increase adrenalin, cortisol and other stress related hormones in the mother's blood, which in turn have an effect on the developing baby. Emerging research shows us that stress in the mother can impact on the infant's development via hypothalamic-pituitary-adrenal pathways in ways that we are yet to fully understand. The hypothalamus and pituitary gland in the brain, and the adrenal glands above the kidneys, are linked by parasympathetic and endocrine pathways and they function in concert in relation to stress and fear. This primal response is more commonly known as the 'fight-flight response'. Armed with this knowledge of stress pathways, we have become more aware that maternal mental state can have an impact on fetal development.

There is new evidence to show that babies look at and respond to their parents from the time of birth. The baby looks at the mother while she holds and feeds the baby and this repeated interaction of looking and responding to the baby's needs is an important part of the bonding process.

The baby's primary experiences are based on the need for survival and the baby's responses are instinctive or reflex. The baby cries when hungry, cold, wet or when she experiences discomfort and this engenders a response of some kind from the parent. When the parent responds in a consistent manner to satisfy the baby's needs, she feels safe. With repeated positive responses from the parent the baby learns through experience that her needs will be met.

The parent's ability to provide for physical needs such as food, warmth and comfort, as well as the emotional needs namely, closeness, safety and reassurance allows the infant to develop trust that these needs will be met. This enhances a sense of security. When the infant's needs are frustrated because there is little, inconsistent or no response on the part of the parent, the risk is that early feelings of insecurity and lack of trust develops.

A relationship is a two way process. If the baby is ill, has developmental problems or sensory difficulties that impede her ability to respond to the parent's attempts to engage the baby, then the interaction between the parent and baby is interrupted. In this situation the parent may be left with feelings of helplessness and impotence in their ability to engender a response from their baby. Support given to the mother by her partner, grandparent or other persons involved can reduce the anxiety or distress that the mother feels in this situation, which in turn enables her to engage with the baby even when the baby is not well or responsive. The role of the family and extended family members cannot be underestimated when it comes to thinking about support for the parents of young children.

The baby's development at an emotional level is dependent on many factors. There are factors innate in the infant, which allow the infant to respond to her parent. These include sensory development (ability to see, hear and touch), physical development (ability to move around and explore the surroundings), and cognitive development (ability to learn through experience and adapt to the environment). Factors in the parent such as their own physical, emotional and mental well-being can have an impact on their interaction with their baby. There are also external factors in the environment that affect the baby/parent unit such as poverty, social disadvantage, family or social instability. All these factors need to be taken into account as we come to understand individual vulnerabilities in children.

Women have traditionally been the primary care-givers, but in many instances fathers are more actively involved in the care of their infants. The sex of the carer is irrelevant when it comes to nurturing the baby. The only difference is the mother's ability to breast-feed the baby. Nursing and cuddling by the father is just as important as the breast-feeding process, when it comes to bonding with the infant. Some women are unable to breast-feed, for a variety of reasons, and bottle-feeding allows the same opportunity for closeness and bonding. What is important is the level of care taken, protection provided and responsiveness given to the baby's needs. These factors will ultimately affect the baby's development of a sense of self in relation to others.

When parents provide for the baby's needs they talk to the baby, smile and coo so that the baby's first social interaction is with her parents. Here the baby learns about social turn taking. The parent initiates a response, the baby watches the parent's smiling face, smiles back at the parent and the behaviour is repeated. Later the baby attempts to imitate the parent's vocal interactions by making babbling sounds. The baby soon learns that an action on her part, for example her smiling, elicits a response from her parent in that the parent gets excited at the first smile, smiles back and the action is repeated. In this way social learning begins and the baby learns that she has some effect on her world and that she is capable of eliciting a response in others.

Where parents respond consistently to the baby, the baby will repeat the action and then move on to trying a different action. Continued learning and interaction with the parents thus occurs and new skills develop. Where parents respond inconsistently or where there is little response to the baby due to the parent's absence or illness, the baby may show distress at first but soon reduces her attempts to engage with the parent and will subsequently withdraw. Therefore the parent's active involvement with their baby from the moment of birth is extremely precious and sets up early patterns for future behaviour, social interaction and learning.

Toddler years

The toddler years span from around 12 months on average when babies begin to walk and move around in their environment, until the age of 2 to 2½ years. Growth occurs rapidly during the first couple of years and brain development also progresses quickly during this time. As toddlers develop, they begin to separate from their parents and test their autonomy in relation to people around them. Every parent who has had their determined toddler repeatedly say 'no' to their requests has knowledge of this normal, although sometimes difficult, stage of development.

The determined and apparently willful behaviour of the toddler is a normal and essential stage of development and it helps parents to realise that the toddler is not deliberately being 'naughty'. If toddlers don't develop this sense of curiosity, which leads them to explore their environment, then their learning and ability to relate to and act within the environment can be impaired. This could result in fearfulness and reluctance at trying new activities.

The toddler stage is where children need to be validated with respect to their wants, needs and behaviour. During this period they need careful monitoring by their parents for physical safety while allowing freedom to explore the environment. Exploration allows for learning about the environment and the objects within that environment. The typical toddler generally explores an area not too far from their parent and will continually check back to see where their parent is. This is not necessarily true of hyperactive toddlers or toddlers who are developmentally delayed, because they are likely explore further without checking back for their parent. As a result, they need much closer parental supervision.

This stage of development is further complicated by the fact that the toddlers cannot easily express their needs verbally and many toddlers have only a few words without complete sentences. This means that their parents often need to work out, by observing their behaviour, what they want or what they are trying to achieve. This can be a challenging but nevertheless rewarding process for their parents, as they see their young child attain steps towards achieving independence. It is beneficial if the parent 'puts into words' the toddler's actions, because this validates the toddler's actions or feelings and engenders the important early experience of feeling understood.

Preschool years

The preschool child learns about socialising by playing alongside and interactively with other children. Playing cooperatively and learning to share is an important process at this time. The young child needs good communication skills to effectively interact with other children and this ability becomes progressively more important as the child grows older. Delay in the language skills of young children may lead to delay in social skills because our primary mode of social interaction with others is through the use of language. Through effective communication skills the young preschool child interacts and connects with other children in play. A positive social interchange occurs when other children respond to the child, which encourages the child to continue to engage in the verbal interaction. Thus the child's expressive language continues to develop and expand.

The child who has delayed language skills may not be able to communicate effectively in this way and may have difficulty engaging other children who have more advanced language skills. This could result in frustration on the part of the child with delayed language and can lead to them 'acting out' their attempts at communication in a physical manner. They may pull, push or hit other children in order to communicate with them. This action could mistakenly be interpreted as aggression.

An adult observing this behaviour might reprimand the child without understanding that he is attempting to interact, although inappropriately, with the other children. Severe or punitive reprimand without this understanding could result in escalation of the physical behaviour, with more apparent aggression, or could result in withdrawal from further attempts to interact socially with other children. Here it is helpful for the adult to observe the behaviour and try to understand the situation. Then the adult can then express in words what the child might be wanting to communicate, but is unable to because of delayed language.

These children benefit from speech and language intervention with a trained therapist to enable them to learn to use language and communicate more effectively. The therapist usually provides parents with techniques for encouraging language and effective non-verbal communication so that the child can get their message through to others.

The preschool years are an important time for learning effective social interaction and communication skills with others, especially with children of the same age, before the child commences school.

2: Experiences and Relationships in Later Childhood

As children mature and develop, their learning becomes more and more influenced by other persons in their environment. The influence of people beyond the nuclear family, such as teachers and friends, becomes more significant to the child. This is a natural process and a necessary part of development for children as they separate from their parents and become more independent in their thinking.

Early school years

The early school aged child is plunged into a world of learning and interaction with others, apart from family members. The child now has to interact with peers in a give and take situation. By this time children have learned about turn taking and sharing in preschool years and will need to exercise this ability more readily during their school years.

The school-aged child will also begin to take more risks. Whilst wanting to separate from the parent, this child still needs the security of knowing that the parent is always there for them. As they explore their world, they may make mistakes and they will need their parents to guide them, teach them and also show faith in them. Recent research has shown the importance of parental involvement during these middle childhood years.

A balance is required between the parent giving the child more freedom to explore other relationships and situations, while providing continuing guidance to the child. Thus the parent remains an important reference point for the child. The parent's own attitudes to life and belief systems will now influence the child's thinking as the child begins to ask more questions. Teachers and others in authority also have a powerful influence at this time. If the child has a warm, positive and healthy relationship with the parent, which has been built up during the precious preschool years, then irrespective of what they hear from others the child will still come back to check with the parent, even if only indirectly.

This is a precious time in the development of the individual where they are beginning to assert themselves and their opinions in relation to others. If the relationship between the parent and child has not been positive during the early years then that child is more likely to lean towards the opinions of others. Where parents have not had positive parenting experiences during their own childhood, the process of raising a young child can be both difficult and challenging.

When the school aged child questions the parent's authority, the parent might feel threatened that the child is no longer following their advice and may try to override the child's ideas with their own opinions. The parent might inadvertently overwhelm the ideas of the child, without understanding where the child is coming from and why they are asking the particular question. This runs the risk of showing a lack of respect for the child's ideas, thoughts and experience. A strictly authoritarian approach rarely leads to positive exchange with children. Instead, children are likely to feel thwarted in their attempts to learn about their world and the adult's lack of respect towards them may make them feel angry and distrusting of adults.

Many insightful parents have been in the position of recognizing the negativity in their interaction with their children and have stepped out bravely to work on their own attitudes and issues. By the parent becoming more enlightened about their own emotions and intentions they in turn learn how their own reactions to the child can be unrelated to the child's experience and therefore might have nothing to do with the situation occurring at the time. By being aware of their own reactions and 'disengaging' these reactions from their interaction with the child, the parent becomes more directly responsive to the child. By disengaging is meant that the parent recognises and separates their fear and anxiety about a situation, from what is actually happening in that moment with their child.

Ultimately, parents who love their children want the best for them and will go to any length to seek help. Essentially, love and respect is the key. Parents do not have to be perfect, but when they act in the best interests of their children based on their love and respect for them, then their children are more likely to develop a healthy sense of self.

Adolescence

The pre-adolescent (about 10–13) and adolescent (about 14 – 18) years provide new challenges for parents. The adolescent is seeking to develop an identity separate to that of their parents and again this is a normal stage of development. Parental opinion is often perceived by the adolescent as less important than that of peers or influential others, and this can be very distressing to parents. The teenager is developing an outward view of the world and begins to move away from parental ideas and influence. The teenager is likely to take on some of the values and beliefs of their parents and discard others.

The adolescent is at the stage of experimenting with issues of right and wrong. The adolescent will often challenge their parents to provoke a response, despite the fact that they may really agree with their parents on some issues. The aim at this stage of development is to question the 'status quo'. The adolescent does not want to accept things merely because they are told. They need to see life in action. This is where our example as parents is of paramount importance.

Where parents tell adolescents not to engage in an activity that they engage in, the chances are that the adolescent will ignore them. When parents indulge in emotional or physical addictions, whatever they may be, they may find that their adolescents engage in similar behaviours. Also, parents cannot expect adolescents to treat them with respect if they do not, in turn, treat them with respect. If adults behave in a rude or arrogant manner towards adolescents then they can expect adolescents to be rude and arrogant towards them.

This stage of development is often the most challenging for parents. The child is physically grown up and in some cases may be physically larger and even stronger than the parent. When the child was younger the parent might have been able to persuade the child to cooperate, but this is often not possible in this age group. Also, some parents feel quite intimidated by the physical stature of their adolescents. A different mode of interaction is required.

This is the stage where parents need to negotiate and discuss important issues with the teenager realizing that they no longer have a direct or even strong influence on the teenager's behaviour, contrary to the case when the individual was younger. It helps if parents develop an environment where they respect the ideas of their teenagers, even if they do not agree with them, and encourage open discussion and negotiation.

Developing contracts with adolescents about rules and parental expectations goes a long way to help parents remain focussed on the important issues and not become overburdened by petty and irrelevant ones. The process of negotiation established in the early school years now provides a basis for a successful interaction with the adolescent.

Where there is a history of positive interaction with the child from an early age during the preschool years, parents are more likely to find that their adolescents continue to have positive interactions with them. Even if they disagree and want to pursue their own way, they are likely to respect parental opinions and guidance. This again stresses the value of fostering good relationships with children early in their lives, and well before they commence school.

As with younger children, consistency and clarity regarding rules and boundaries enables adolescents to respond within these boundaries or negotiate rules in a healthy and positive manner. Rules and boundaries will need to change as children mature, but parents need to be clear about these rule changes and why they are implemented. Parents may also find that adolescents are more responsive when they communicate their concerns in a positive manner.

Teenagers are quick to pick holes in ideas or beliefs that are held rigidly without clarity and conviction. Parents need self-awareness and have a good basis for the rules and guidance they give when dealing with adolescents. The notion of 'doing as you are told' without good reason is unlikely to work with teenagers.

Open discussion about rules and boundaries with agreement to disagree on some issues may be required. Importantly, there should be the recognition that the parent has to maintain the final say, particularly where the adolescent's behaviour places them at risk of harm. The trust built up over years of good communication between the parent and child comes to fruition in adolescence, because the adolescent has learned that their parents make decisions in their best interest.

As with the younger child it is not a major catastrophe when parents make mistakes unintentionally in interacting with adolescents, provided they remain honest and apologize to the adolescent when appropriate. Apologizing to children does not mean that they are given free rein. It means that the parent is willing to reconsider opinions or actions in situations where the parent has been inadvertently unfair in laying down the rules.

Encouraging dialogue and open communication with adolescents makes them feel that they will be heard, which goes a long way in fostering positive interactions. Fair and reasoned guidance from their parents encourages the adolescent to make better decisions and better choices.

3: The Importance of the Preschool Years

Children develop a sense of self-worth based on their experience of self and this development occurs at various stages and to varying degrees. When young children receive a positive response from their parent for a particular behaviour then they are likely to repeat the behaviour so as to continue the positive response. Children develop a sense of their abilities initially based on their parent's response. As they grow older, responses from other persons in authority to the child, such as extended family members and teachers, become more important.

The sense of self and identity continues to develop during the school years and during adolescence. During the latter stage in particular, the responses from parents have less impact and here the opinions of peers and other influential figures, such as that of their teachers, become more important. Therefore it is imperative that the parental-child bonding occurs early in the child's life or the parent runs the risk of trying to connect with the child at a stage when the child has already begun to move away from parental influence.

Time spent with young preschool children developing a secure and trusting relationship is of great importance for the development of healthy self-esteem, and it also fosters the bond between the parent and the child.

Important aspects in early learning

1. Respect
When the parent responds in a respectful manner to the child, thereby taking the child's feelings about a situation into account, the child learns that their opinions are valued and are considered worthwhile. Even if the child is grossly

mistaken about an idea, the child's comments and thoughts need consideration. To tell children that they are 'silly' or 'stupid' when they make a particular comment is to undervalue their thinking and they then run the risk of believing that their opinion is not valid or important. The response on the part of the parent needs to occur in a sensitive, positive and encouraging manner. Where parents deal sensitively with their children's needs they are bound to raise sensitive children who will respond sensitively to the needs of others.

The home environment is where the child experiences essential lessons in human relationships. The child learns within the home from a very early age how to relate, respond and deal with other human beings. Therefore as parents we need to be aware of our influence during these impressionable preschool years and especially that our children learn from our example. We cannot expect our children to respect us if we do not respect them. Where parents engage in undesirable behaviour, children are likely to copy that behaviour because they inadvertently learn that such behaviour is acceptable.

An authoritarian attitude that 'children should be seen and not heard', or that 'children should do as they are told', sends a powerful message to the developing personality that their ideas and thoughts are not relevant. The child learns that unless they do exactly as their parents tell them they will not be loved. In this situation the parental love is experienced by the child as conditional and significantly hampers the development of self-worth, and consequently self-confidence.

Children need to be given the same respect and consideration that we give to our friends and other adults. They deserve our respect and our honest communication with them.

2. Apology is not about 'giving in' to the child

It is not a perfect world and we all make mistakes. Parents become tired at the end of a long, busy day and may not respond in a positive manner to their children despite their best intentions. When parents make mistakes in relating with their child, it is important that they talk to them and apologize to the child where the parent was in the wrong.

Children brought up within a loving environment want very much to please their parents and if they see that their parent has been unfair, but is prepared to apologize, they readily and willingly forgive them. Children usually very much want happiness and stability in their home environment. Consequently, they will often forgive their parents even for the most unreasonable behaviour on the parent's part, in order to move on from the painful issue and return the situation to normal.

3. Trust develops early

It is vital to remember how important the young child views this primary relationship with their parent.

The parent-child relationship is disrupted if the parent does not respect the child and deals harshly or aggressively with the child. The child can then no longer afford to invest too much emotion in the relationship with that parent for fear of upsetting the parent and being unfairly reprimanded. The relationship with that parent then suffers and the reduced trust can mean that the child is unlikely to communicate well with that parent in later years. If the parent inadvertently behaves unfairly towards the child an apology might be necessary.

It is important to recognise that the sense of trust and security in the child-parent relationship needs to develop early in the child's preschool experience. When this does not occur there is the risk that the child might not trust that parent or their guidance in future years.

4. The child's trust means greater responsibility for the parent

In view of their emotional vulnerability and their need to feel secure, young children are innately vulnerable to events in their environment. Loving parents readily engender trust in their children, but when parental behaviour is unpredictable, manipulative or punitive the child cannot develop a wholesome trust.

Parents therefore have enormous responsibility regarding the trust and vulnerability of their children and must avoid manipulating their children in order to fulfil their own needs. Self-knowledge on the part of parents enables them to separate their issues from the needs of their children.

5. Bright young children can be challenging

Cognitive development in all children varies widely. Brighter and more socially advanced children will require positive experiences in relating with their parents at an earlier age than typically developing peers. Bright young children may appear to be more demanding of their parents' time and attention, and are often not content to be left alone without stimulation or interaction of some kind.

When dealing with the behaviour of bright and demanding children, their parents need to respond to their behaviour in a firm, yet clear and instructive manner probably at a much earlier age than many of their peers. These children often appear to be more demanding because they usually enjoy stimulation and like to be kept busy.

Raising bright children can be challenging for their parents. It is important that parents remain in charge and not give the control to the child. Both parents need to work together on child-rearing issues and should try to not undermine each other, because the bright child will easily sense this rift.

Also, parents will need to apply negotiation techniques at an earlier age with bright children. Typically, negotiation starts in the preschool years just before commencing school and should be fairly well established during the early school years. However, with the bright child these methods may need to be applied much earlier. See the following chapter for more on this subject.

Importantly, not all bright children display challenging behaviour. Individual personality comes into play. Some bright children may be reserved, quiet and more introverted in personality and they may be content to entertain themselves without making undue demands on their parents.

Conclusion

Spending time with young children, showing interest in their activities while guiding their behaviour is a valuable part of the preschool experience.

The preschool child deserves the same respect that is given to older children. The communication style might be simpler but must not be dismissed as less important.

Where parents recognize that they get things wrong and admit this to their children by sitting down and discussing this with them at the level that the child can understand, they go a long way in nurturing the relationship with their children.

It's been said by many that children are our future and as parents we have a powerful opportunity to influence the future by interacting with our children in a positive, loving and respectful manner.

4: Self-concept, Self-esteem and Self-image

It is well recognized that self-esteem is an important determinant of personal achievement. Individuals who lack self-esteem have little or no belief in their abilities and this presents outwardly as lack of confidence. It may be helpful, for the purpose of this book, to define what is meant by self-concept, self- esteem and self- image.

Definitions

Self-image is what we wish others to see about ourselves. It is the part of ourselves that we project to the outside world and it does not necessarily represent a complete or true picture of that which we inwardly hold about ourselves. Self-image is how we want others to see us in relation to other people or in different situations. We may have a predominantly negative self-concept with acute awareness of our weaknesses and there may be aspects of ourselves that we are ashamed about, but we may still manage to project an image of confidence. The difficulty here is that this image is just a veneer. The image has no depth and can easily be eroded by events or conflicts in our interactions with others. Therefore our self-image is not necessarily a true reflection of what we think or feel about ourselves.

Self-esteem is how we feel about ourselves and is predominantly emotionally based. When we do good deeds for others or when we succeed in our goals, we feel good about ourselves and we have confidence to try the gesture or the activity again next time. That is, we have positive self-esteem in relation to that particular activity. Self-esteem, although mostly based on how we feel about ourselves, is also based on our inner awareness and knowledge about ourselves and is therefore closely linked to our self-concept.

Consequently, the same factors involved in the development of our self-concept affect our self-esteem as well.

Self-concept is our inner perception of who we are and is mostly a cognitive or thinking state. It is essentially knowledge and experience based and it gives us a sense of who we are. This rest of this chapter will focus on self-concept as the primary step in developing healthy self-esteem and it is important when considering the development of young children.

Development of Self-concept

What is self-concept?

Self-concept is our inner perception of ourselves and relates to what we really think about ourselves. It is based on self-knowledge, self-recognition and self-acceptance. As we develop we come to know ourselves, accept ourselves and love ourselves and consequently we develop a strong self-concept.

As we move through life we learn about our individual strengths and weaknesses and this knowledge, based on our experience, helps to build our self-concept. Therefore our experiences can significantly impact on our self-concept. If we have predominantly positive experiences in the development of our self-concept we can expect to have a predominantly positive self-concept and therefore positive self-esteem. Negative experiences do impinge on our self-concept in the same way, but it depends on the degree to which our self-concept has become firmly established as to whether the negative experiences will have a lasting negative effect.

Building positive self-concept begins in infancy when the parent responds positively to the child's needs, as described in the first chapter. Subsequently, the way in which persons in our environment respond to us and nurture us, influences the continued development of our early self-concept. With time and development comes experience and this further influences the development of our self-concept.

Even individuals with a healthy, positive self-concept will in certain circumstances feel vulnerable and experience weakening of their self-esteem and confidence. The challenge for all of us is that we learn from our experiences. We learn about our response to difficult situations and then we move forward with a positive belief in ourselves that we will cope better next time.

It is essential that we do not negatively reprimand ourselves over and over again for our mistakes, as we may be inclined give up and then cannot be bothered trying again the next time round. Learning invariably involves making mistakes and this recognition is important in the process of our development. These same principles apply to our children and the development of their self-concept.

Loving ourselves is an essential component in the development of healthy self- concept. We may erroneously believe that it is not good to love ourselves or to love ourselves too much. Yet in all wise teachings it is often stated that unless we love ourselves we cannot love another.

If we are unable to accept ourselves unconditionally we cannot accept another unconditionally. If we find our own weaknesses intolerable then we will not be able to tolerate weaknesses in others. Recognizing our weaknesses and mistakes and being willing to learn from them allows us to make better choices next time. We need to be willing to learn from our errors and move forward positively with the belief in ourselves that we will do better next time. This is how we love ourselves and develop a healthy self-concept.

Loving ourselves also incorporates having respect for ourselves and therefore respect for others. Love involves taking responsibility for our actions. When acting lovingly towards ourselves we also act responsibly towards ourselves. In the same way we extend love and responsibility towards others.

What influences the development of our self-concept?

1. Nurturing environment

A healthy self-concept develops when an individual feels nurtured. The developing individual thrives in a loving and supportive environment where love is directed at the individual and where love is evident within that environment. In Western Society, our parents generally provide the emotional and physical environment in which we grow. However, in other societies extended family members or members of the community play a more significant role. For the purposes of discussion, reference is made to parents, but any primary carer, carers or others involved in the raising of the child can be substituted.

Young children, at first, learn about themselves in relation to the effect that they have on those around them. If children's efforts are praised, if they are encouraged in activities and interests, if they are accepted for who they are and do not have to 'win' their parent's love and acceptance, then they are on the path to developing self-love.

When children feel threatened, when their efforts are not acknowledged and when they are constantly told that they are stupid or are made to feel unworthy, they are at serious risk of developing poor self-concept. Children need to experience love, respect and kindness in order to develop healthy self-concept.

2. Experience is key

It is necessary to say that healthy self-concept is based on truth. Where the child knows that he is not good at a particular activity, but everyone around him tells him that he is, he cannot develop a positive concept of himself in relation to that activity. Experience is the key. In order for the child to truly develop a positive concept he needs to experience himself as successful in that activity so that his concept of success is based on his positive experience.

The experience allows success at an activity to become reality for the child. Therefore it is beneficial to tap into our children's strengths and to positively encourage the development of their individual talents so that they can experience success at these tasks. Where they have no genuine interest in an activity, and are merely forced to do it because of parental or another person's expectations, then they cannot develop an experience of success with that activity.

Experience is different for everyone. No two people experience the same event in the same way. Therefore the experience of success is different for all of us. If the child experiences himself as successful based on his own efforts then he is successful in that particular situation. This of course becomes difficult to apply when we consider activities where there is some yardstick, or preset measure, that has to be surpassed in order to succeed.

3. Success is an individual process

Too often success is based on winning and on being number one. Yet success is just as great for the individual who has tried and practiced so hard that merely crossing the finish line in a race is reward, as for the individual who is first to cross the line.

Where children are participating in any activity that inherently involves competition, they should be encouraged to set their *own* targets and goals, rather than comparing themselves to others and the achievements of others. We then encourage them to develop an internal measure of success based on their own goals and achievements, and they learn that their success is not measured by comparison to the achievements of others.

4. Values and beliefs determine perception of success

We refer to success, but what does it mean to be successful? Our belief about success is based on what we are taught. We may have learned at a young age that to be successful is to have material goals that result in material gains, for example financial wealth, that reflect our success. Then this will be the type of success that we will aspire to.

Alternatively, we may learn that success is about having positive relationships with all people that we come into contact with in our daily life, and that success is about contributing in some way to the wellbeing of our fellow men. In this instance, we develop a totally different view of success. The latter form of success cannot easily be measured and may not produce obvious physical results, whereas the former is often clearly quantifiable and is visible for all to see.

When we examine the qualities of great leaders, cooperative cohesive workers and individuals who reach out to help others, we see the characteristics of success that cannot be measured in material gains. Instead we see the positive effects that these individuals have on the lives of other people.

5. Self-concept develops over time

As children mature, their self-concept develops based on their experiences. At first this characteristic is influenced by those closest to them, essentially their families, but over time their experience of life extends beyond the family and these later experiences influence what they ultimately think about themselves.

Where we experience positive feelings about ourselves, as a result of how others react to us, we begin to think positively about ourselves and our self-concept continues to develop in a positive way. Negative experiences will occur, but when we have a strong belief in ourselves based on past experience, they do not erode our self-concept and confidence in ourselves.

There is no end to the development of children's self-concept, which continues to evolve as they continue to grow, make mistakes, have success and learn about themselves through their experiences in life.

Conclusion

The values and beliefs of our parents, teachers and community leaders influence, not only their own lives, but also the lives of young people growing up under their guidance. Thus parents and carers of young children have an enormous responsibility in promoting the development of emotionally healthy fellow human beings.

The next chapter will discuss ways in which healthy self-concept can be encouraged and nurtured.

5: Encouraging the development of a healthy self-concept

There are many requirements for the development of healthy self-concept and some of the key requirements, in my view, are discussed in this chapter. They include:

1. Love

2. Guidance

3. Belief and positive expectation

1. Love

Love is experienced by all of us in many different ways. At the physical level, love is experienced through the provision of food, warmth and safe place to live. At the emotional level, love is experienced through emotional nurturing and support. And at the mental level, love is experienced through recognition and respect for the individual. All these aspects of love need attention for young children to thrive and grow.

We are familiar with the many qualities of love as they are often referred to in wise teachings. The key qualities of love that promote the development of healthy self-concept are:

- Love is unconditional. Unconditional love does not require perfection, obligation or submission. It surrounds the developing individual like an invisible cloak and allows the individual to develop to the best of their potential.
- Love makes no demands of the individual, and does not require the individual to conform to any preconceived ideas. Love wants only what is best for the loved individual.

- Love accepts the individual as is, without exception. Love may recognize the faults or errors in behaviour, but does not focus on them. Instead love encourages the individual to try again, to do better next time and gives positive recognition for the effort.
- Love is nurturing, supportive and is always present. It can be relied on in good and bad times.
- Love requires no reward or payback. The mere ability to witness the healthy growth of the loved individual is love's best reward. Love does not demand or require any obligations or acts of duty.
- Love exists purely for love's sake. Love extends itself towards the one that is loved and towards others because it knows of no other way to exist.

Love and the developing child

Children thrive in the presence of love. When children are loved they feel accepted for who they are, their needs are fulfilled and they are respected as individuals. We all know the powerful effects of love. Love motivates us, gives us strength and love gives us belief in ourselves to reach out and to develop to our best potential. Love makes us want to please the person who loves us. The same is true for our children. Where the child has a loving and trusting relationship with an adult, the child will work hard not to disappoint that adult. The adult who gives unconditional love to a child develops a strong and enduring relationship with that child.

The importance of love in the development of a young child should never be underestimated. Even where the child does not appear successful by external measures, the child who is loved, thrives emotionally and develops a healthy self-concept. The child who is loved is encouraged to be the best person that they can be, while at the same time the child is always loved just for being who they are. This in turn leads to the development of an individual who has a strong belief in themselves, which then carries them through life and gives them the inner strength and ability to ride the rough times.

Therefore, loving our children also means that we want what is best for them. We nurture, support and respect them so that they can develop to the best of their potential.

2. Guidance

Children need the guidance of their parents, carers or elders, if they are to cope with life and live happily. Their parents teach them the skills for surviving and coping in the social environment with other people. Children need guidance about the basic values of right and wrong from their parents and carers. They cannot be left to develop these without guidance by a loving parent or caregiver, because they do not have the experiences in life to call upon.

Religions and cultural traditions have for a long time taught the basic concepts of right and wrong and many of these constructs provide rules and a framework for behaviour that is taught to be right or wrong for that particular culture or society. Irrespective of religion, children need to have basic rules or codes that govern their behaviour, so that they can live peacefully and cooperatively with their fellow human beings in a social environment.

Through guidance we teach our children moral values based on our own beliefs and experience. Some of these values that I believe are important include:

- The sanctity of human life and that we cannot take the life of another human being
- Respect for another person's property and that we should not steal another's possessions
- Respect for the basic human rights of each individual

- The importance of taking responsibility for our behaviour and recognizing that our behaviour has an impact on others
- Respect for all living things: plant and animal
- Respect for and appreciation of nature
- Appreciation of the balance of life and the cyclical nature of life; that we cannot do an act to another without there being some consequence which will affect us later; that what we do to others we ultimately do to ourselves
- Appreciation for the interconnectedness of all living things; respect for our environment and our planet; respect for the delicate balance of nature
- Understanding the power and influence of love in everything that we do, at work or play

As we pass these values to our children we need to be clear in our own minds about the reasons for our beliefs because our children will ask questions and may challenge us. If we have strong and clear reasons based on honesty about our own experiences, our children will be satisfied. However, if we believe in something merely because we have been told, or if we have beliefs based on guilt or fear of retribution, then our children are less likely to be satisfied or be inclined to follow our teaching.

3. Belief and positive expectation

Children need their parents and loved ones to believe in them. Even when they flounder and make mistakes, they need to trust that their inner strength and ability will see them through the difficult times. However, they cannot develop a sense of their inner strength if they experience that the adults in their life are afraid for them and have a sense of doom about their future.

The way we think about our children has a powerful effect on their behaviour. If we expect our children to fail and falter, they may tune in to our feelings because our behavior towards them has changed. Consequently, our children's ability to think positively about themselves may be hindered.

Our thoughts, not our words, influence our behaviour. Our words are not nearly as powerful as our thoughts. Even where we profess a belief in our children's ability but we continue to hold strong doubts inwardly, our children are likely to pick up these non-verbal cues. Children are often more perceptive than we think.

Therefore as parents we need to nurture the strengths within our children and then 'have faith' in them. We need to know that with the positive love and guidance that we have given them over the years they will flourish and develop their own talents and abilities. We also need to accept that they will develop these abilities in their own way and not necessarily in the way that we think they should.

Our children may fail, make mistakes and may even experience depression because of their perceived failure. If we as parents, have loved them, nurtured them and supported them through their early developing years then we need to trust that they will call on their own inner strength to see them through the difficult times. During these times they will know that their parents will be there to support them.

As parents we need to avoid feeling overwhelmed ourselves when our children experience tough times, which means we will need to call on our own inner strength as well. At these times we particularly need to have faith and believe that our children will come through the situation, while we help and support them to deal with it. Where our children sense that we are afraid and feel overwhelmed, they cannot trust their own strength as effectively. They model themselves on our behaviour. They can feel strong if they see that we feel strong and believe in them.

We, as parents and carers, know that we cannot always shelter our children from hurt or harm because many events are out of our control. However, we need to understand that our children will need to live and experience their lives in their own way. Our help and support will be there for them during the tough times. It is by going through the tough times that our children develop confidence in their own inner strength and abilities, which in turn helps them to learn and grow.

6: Dealing with children's behaviour

1. Rules and boundaries are important

We all have rules and boundaries that govern our behaviour. In order for society to function in a cohesive manner the rules that govern the society need to be known and followed. Children first learn about rules and boundaries in the home environment. They need to know the rules within the household and then they need clear boundaries that govern their behaviour.

Without rules and boundaries children have free rein. They can do as they wish without learning to contain their urges and control their impulses. Where there are clear boundaries with guidelines from their parents about what they expect from their children, young children are able to learn to control their own behaviour. Children also feel more secure in an environment where there is structure and clear rules, because then they know what is expected of them.

What is the age for teaching rules?

The age for teaching young children about boundaries and rules is at around the time that the child develops physical autonomy, which is generally around one year of age, but it might be earlier in children with advanced motor skills. This is a time when children are learning to exert their own will and it is also at this time that they test their will against that of their parents. Consequently, tantrums in the toddler years are not infrequent and are a normal stage of development during this early stage of developing independence.

Gentle guidance with the parent dealing firmly and consistently with the young child in a non-punitive and respectful manner, enables the child to learn about rules and boundaries. It is important at this stage to recognize that exploration of the environment by touching and examining objects is a normal stage of development and it is best to remove dangerous items from the child's reach rather than persistently telling them 'don't touch'.

It becomes significantly more difficult for children to learn about rules later, if they are given total freedom in preschool years and are then expected to conform to rules when they commence school. In the same way, expecting a pre-adolescent or adolescent to be cooperative with rules is unrealistic if the individual has never had to learn to conform to rules and boundaries within the family home during the early years.

What if there are no rules?

In the absence of boundaries and rules, children are likely to 'push to the limits' to see how much they can get away with. Therefore it is important for parents to communicate clear, consistent yet fair rules that children can follow within the home. This is the first step in learning to function effectively in relation to other people. Importantly, parents must agree on the rules within the family home and not work against each other.

If children do not learn about rules, boundaries and expectations for behaviour within the family home, they are at risk of becoming self-centred and are more likely to have difficulty with conforming to rules outside the family home.

What about contracts and negotiation?

Parents can work out a contract with their children about the behaviours and the cooperation that they expect, so that when children break the rules they have a clear understanding of the consequences and punishment that they are likely to experience. Contractual arrangements regarding behaviour are more likely to be effective in school age children.

Many preschool children have not yet learned to be objective about their behaviour and may not have the level of understanding that is necessary to develop a contract for their behaviour. This however depends on the cognitive level of development of the child, as very bright preschoolers may be able to cooperate within a contract of rules quite well.

All preschool children understand very clearly and learn quickly about consequences for unacceptable behaviour. Where their acceptable behaviour is reinforced in a positive manner and where there is consistency on the part of their parents when dealing with negative behaviours, children are more likely to learn to modify their behaviour so that they become more cooperative.

What about stifling the child's creativity?

The presence of rules and boundaries does not preclude the development of creativity in the mind of the young child. When children feel secure and loved, they have room for the creativity to grow and blossom. Creativity flows in a relaxed and stress-free environment.

In the absence of rules and boundaries children are likely to continue to test their parent's limits, and this in turn leads to stress and exhaustion on the part of the parent. In this environment creativity is less likely to blossom.

It is mistakenly thought that children should be given freedom to develop and explore without clear guidelines from their parents about rules and expectations for behaviour. This leads to later problems with behaviour that could be difficult to stem in the long term.

2. Reinforcement of behaviour

Young children thrive on positive encouragement and attention that they get from their parents and carers, especially in a loving and supportive environment. When they receive praise for their efforts they will repeat their efforts and thus their positive behaviour is reinforced. If they receive attention for unacceptable behaviour the chances are that they will repeat the behaviour even though their parents may not approve of that behaviour. Ultimately, the child seeks parental approval and attention. If the child cannot get the approval, then attention, even without approval, is the next best thing for the child.

Behaviour management techniques stress the importance of giving attention to positive and acceptable behaviour while ignoring the inappropriate and negative ones. Before ignoring the negative behaviour, it is important to address the behaviour. Briefly explain to the child what it is about the behaviour that is negative and then provide them with a more positive and constructive way for them to express what they want. In this way the parent can respond to the child's request if reasonable, before deeming the behaviour as negative. Then the child can be told that if the negative behaviour persists despite the explanation, that it will be ignored and there will be consequences. Consequences usually include removal of privileges.

The aim of allowing the child to make a request and explain what they are doing helps to avoid misunderstanding. Simply ignoring all negative behaviours, without checking the issue and telling the child what you expect, can lead to the negative behaviours escalating in order to get attention. Then the more the behaviour is ignored, the more the child escalates the behaviour. This is the dynamic of temper tantrums, which can occur in older children if they are not given an opportunity to express what they want or if they are not given a chance to explain the issue to their parent.

This approach pays respect to the child's needs without letting them get away with bad behaviour. If the child is told to *'listen to me'* by the parent, but the parents fails to listen to the child, then miscommunication occurs and the child could become increasingly frustrated. Giving time for the child to explain what they want also encourages the child *'to think'* about what they are doing and *'to think'* about how their behaviour affects others.

The child who has a positive relationship with the parent is more likely to want both approval and attention from the parent and is therefore more compliant in behaviour. Where the child is in a loving and supportive relationship with the parent, often the parent's lack of approval alone will generally ensure that the child will not repeat the behaviour.

3. Consequences for unacceptable behaviour

When children do not cooperate despite the parent making it verbally clear what is expected of them, they need to be told that there will be consequences if the behaviour continues. If the uncooperative behaviour persists then consequences, such as removal of privileges, will need to be carried out in a consistent manner. The consequences that are applied will need to vary depending on the child's age, interests or perceived desires.

What about a little slap to control behaviour?

Physical reprimand in any manner as a form of discipline is strongly discouraged, as this engenders aggression and fear in the child. Children that are hit or that observe hitting within the home are more likely to hit others and become physically aggressive over time.

As children are physically smaller and vulnerable, hitting them is harsh and runs the risk of physically hurting the child. When the parent hits the child the parent has invariably lost control of their feelings of anger and frustration in that situation. The child will sense that loss of control.

Punishments instead could be in the form of removal of privileges and time out. Where parents have difficulty with instituting time out or similar techniques, it is beneficial to obtain support and guidance with a child psychologist, a community health team or a paediatrician.

Keep the child informed about the reason for the discipline

When using discipline with children, keep them informed and involved about the issue that they are being disciplined for. However, a long explanation at the time of the incident is not appropriate as it is likely to diffuse the impact of the punishment.

Once the child has had time out and has settled down so as to be more cooperative, then time can be spent with the child to talk about the issues in order to help them learn where they have gone wrong. They can then be told what they could have done to avoid the need for punishment, which encourages them to think and behave differently in the future. In this way they learn from their mistakes. It also helps to engage the child in an acceptable activity in which they are likely to succeed, in order to divert them from the unacceptable behaviour or activity.

Encourage your child's ability to think about their behaviour and the impact that it has on others. Recognise that sometimes children do silly things without thinking and they might not willfully have meant any harm. The process of encouraging the child to 'think about what you have done', once the dust has settled, enables the child to develop the ability to reflect on their behaviour and to learn from silly mistakes.

Importantly however, we cannot expect young children to learn from their mistakes if we do not provide them with guidance regarding their behaviour.

Remain calm and in control of your emotions

We need to avoid cajoling and begging our children to cooperate with us, as this puts them in the position of strength. A begging or cajoling parent is not in control of the situation and the child will sense this quickly.

Speak the rules clearly, simply and honestly to children and make sure that they have received the message. Remain in charge or else the child might unwittingly try to manipulate the situation. A calm, firm manner and a serious voice often goes a long way to making it clear that you mean what you say.

Avoid high-pitched shouting as this sends the message that you have lost control. Also, avoid joking or laughing about the situation because then the child does not learn to take parental discipline techniques seriously. It is unwise to smile, or comment on 'how cute' the young child is when they are having a tantrum because this renders the discipline as ineffective and could lead to the child ignoring parental discipline the next time round.

Parents must work together

Both parents need to work together to set the rules and boundaries. Where parents disagree about the rules, the children are likely to play parents against each other, and this makes any attempts to discipline their behaviour ineffective.

It is necessary for parents to discuss the rules and boundaries within the household between themselves before attempting to use them with the children. Parents need to be clear with each other about values, morals and rules before they attempt to discipline their children. In this way they can support each other and form a united front when children misbehave.

Stay in the present

Parents need to deal with behavioural issues in the moment. It is unwise to try to discipline behaviours that occurred days or weeks ago as this will not make sense to the child and the discipline is likely to appear unfair. More importantly the child is unlikely to learn from behaviours that occurred some time ago.

Remain focused on the issues in the present that led to the inappropriate behaviour and help the child to see what they have done wrong. Allow them to give their point of view once they are calm and cooperating, but make it clear that there is no excuse for wrongdoing.

Once dealt with, move on

Once the behaviour has been dealt with appropriately, move on and avoid going over issues that are long in the past. Failure to do so makes the child feel helpless because their negative behaviours of the past are not forgiven and are constantly hanging over their head. This results in negativity in the mind of the child as they can never win and can never please their parent.

Internalization of parental guidance

As children grow and develop, they internalize the attitudes, beliefs and teachings of their parents. Where there is a healthy relationship with the child, the child internalizes the parent's healthy attitudes and teachings. Consequently, when this child misbehaves, they realize that the behaviour is unacceptable to the parent even without the parent having to repeatedly reprimand the child. This development of the 'internalized parent' may be hindered in a child who has developmental problems.

The child with special needs

There are specific difficulties relating to the child with developmental problems and it may be even more challenging for parents to deal with difficult behaviours, because the usual parenting techniques are often not effective. However, the simple principle of always treating children with respect goes a long way in fostering good communication with them.

In the circumstance of a child with developmental problems, the parents may benefit from professional counselling and support, to enable them to best deal with behavioural difficulties in their child.

Love and respect for children

When using discipline techniques with children, we need to remember to remain loving and respectful of our children, even when their behaviour is driving us mad. Distinguish between the child that we love and the behaviour that is unacceptable.

Avoid negative name-calling or typecasting the child as being hopeless, bad or useless, as this will undermine the child's self-esteem. Typecasting also means that the child can never move away from the image that the parent imposed on that child. For example, if we say things like *'oh, he is the difficult one in the family'* or *'she is always arrogant and rude'*, then that child cannot move on and develop different ways of acting or behaving.

By applying a typecast to the child, they will never be acknowledged for trying to do things better the next time. Even if the child tried harder the next time there is still the chance that with typecasting, their parents will continue to see them in a negative light. The child in this position will eventually stop trying, and might become rebellious and even disrespectful toward their parents.

Parental self awareness is important

Parents need to be constantly aware of how they interact with their children. We must avoid using negative labels with our children, which bind them up in such a way that they cannot become free of the negative image that we hold of them.

When we hold on to these images they are usually based on our tendency to stand in judgement of our children. When we judge our children we are not extending love towards them. Instead we are making them feel guilty or worse still, inadequate. We need to continually treat our children with love and respect.

Nurturing positive and sensitive human beings

By loving and respecting our children we encourage the development of caring, cooperative and responsible individuals who have their own special purpose on this planet.

This quotation from The Prophet by Kahlil Gibran provides an insight:

'Your children are not your children. They are the sons and daughters of Life's longing for itself. They come through you but not from you, And though they are with you yet they belong not to you. You may give them your love but not your thoughts, For they have their own thoughts.'

7: Responsibility and Bullying

Teaching children about responsibility

As we develop and mature we learn to take responsibility for our behaviour and our children need to learn the same lesson. Even young preschool children learn quickly about the consequences of their behaviour. This is an important step in their development because it encourages children to think about their actions and to pay attention to how their actions affect others. They can then learn that when they perform an act, it leads to a particular consequence. With guidance and encouragement from their parents they learn how they can take responsibility for their behaviour and change the outcome by changing their actions.

As parents we have to be careful not to make excuses for our children's bad behaviour. If they have done wrong to another, they need to have this pointed out to them, not 'swept under the carpet' hoping that it will go away, because they need to learn that there are consequences to their behaviour. This means that they need to accept responsibility for what they have done and apologize when they have done wrong to another individual. Children fail to develop responsibility if their parents make excuses for them.

Individuals who do not develop personal responsibility continually blame others for their predicaments. They also fail to learn that they have the power to change the course of events in their own lives by altering their own thinking and thus their behaviour. As children develop, they can be encouraged to think about their actions and can learn that their own thinking affects their behaviour. By having predominantly positive and caring thoughts in a situation, the child is more likely to act in a positive and caring manner towards others. The child learns through guidance to stop and think about the consequences of their behaviour and how it will affect others, before they act.

Importantly, the more influence we have on others, the greater is our burden of responsibility towards them. These are lessons that children can learn in their daily interactions with others. If we perceive that we are strong, then we have a greater responsibility to help and assist those that we perceive to be weaker.

The issue of bullying

Bullying is an issue that many children have to deal with, either as perpetrators or as victims. Those who bully others assume that they have some right or power over the needs of others and when they bully they develop a false sense of strength. Yet the truly strong individual is the one who reaches out to protect others and who does not need to prove anything to their peers, because inwardly they know that they are strong. Individuals who bully others need to learn that they have some responsibility for the well-being of others.

Lesson for the bully

Children who bully other children need to learn that what they do to others they ultimately do to themselves. When they hurt another, deep down they know that they have done wrong and this knowledge will continually be on their mind. Therefore by hurting others physically, emotionally or mentally, they hurt themselves because they disturb their own peace of mind.

Children are generally receptive to learning the lessons that life teaches them, but they need the guidance from their parents and carers to point out these lessons. In this way they learn to become more aware of their own behaviour and how it impacts on others. These lessons are best learned in the home environment well before the child commences school, but require continual reinforcement throughout childhood and into young adulthood.

Lesson for the victim

The victims of bullying need to learn a lesson as well. Theirs is one of self-respect and inner knowledge about who they are as individuals. They need to acknowledge their inner strength to help them during times when they are being unfairly treated.

They need to learn that what others say or think about them is not nearly as important as what they believe and know to be true about themselves. Where others are being deliberately unkind to them, they need to remain strong in the knowledge that they are good individuals and that they do not need the approval of others.

Often the victims of bullying act afraid or intimidated. The individual needs to know that they do not deserve to be bullied and no one deserves to be bullied. Tuning in to inner strength enables them to feel stronger mentally, if not physically.

The bullied child can also learn to ignore the persecutions of the bully, and in fact they will soon learn to pity the bully. Individuals who bully others are often victims of bullies themselves. Victims of bullies can become aware that the bully usually lacks an inner sense of strength and tries subconsciously to overcome this insecurity by acts that outwardly display verbal or physical strength.

Counselling is needed

Children who bully others need counselling and support to teach them about fairness, justice and responsibility. Children who are bullied need counselling about self-worth and inner confidence.

Many schools have programs in place to deal with bullying. This is a necessary and important intervention to assist young children who are either the victims or perpetrators of bullying. Dealing with the issue in childhood means that individuals are less likely to continue to be perpetrators or victims of bullying into adulthood.

8: Our communication with our children

This chapter addresses some ideas about communicating in a positive manner with children to enable us to develop an open and honest environment in which children can learn and thrive emotionally.

Words have power

When communicating with children we need to remain aware that the words we use and the way in which we use them can have a powerful effect. If we say one thing whilst meaning the opposite, or if we make a statement about something that we ourselves do not believe, our children will usually pick up on our non-verbal cues. As mentioned earlier, our thoughts have a powerful effect on our behaviour. If we try to suppress our inner feelings, we may become anxious and ill at ease, and these cues may be detectable to others including our children.

We need to be aware that if we hold negative thoughts or fears for our children they will invariably pick up those vibes, and may become fearful themselves. On a daily basis we need to remain as positive and as honest as we can in our communication with our children. Our thoughts are powerful.

If we repeatedly use negative statements that undermine their confidence and that make them feel unworthy of our praise and our love, then our children are likely to feel insecure and not develop confidence in themselves. When this happens they may take on the attitude that they don't care what we think.

Being aware of our thoughts and insecurities

If we hold negative thoughts regarding any issue when dealing with our children then we need to examine them closely to see if they are really applicable in that situation or if they are based on our own fears and insecurities. This is no easy task because we need to separate in our mind whether the fear or feelings we hold is based on our own negative experiences, or whether it is really relevant to the situation involving our child. Sometimes discussion with another adult, friend or family member, can help us to resolve the issue in our minds.

We help our children when we do not burden them with our insecurities and fears that really do not belong to them. Burdening them with our insecurities and fears is likely to undermine the development of their self-esteem and self-confidence.

Being truthful

The old adage 'be true to yourself' is very applicable in our communication with our children. We need to be clear in our own hearts about our beliefs, our motives and our prejudices before we can communicate these to our children. Again this is no easy task. It takes time for us, even as adults, to develop our own ideas about various issues and in many instances we may feel that we do not have an answer. It is OK to tell our children that we don't know the answers and that we are still working on the idea or issue for ourselves. Our children are more likely to respect us if we show them that we are comfortable with not having all the answers. We might even suggest that we work on an issue together with our children.

Being sensitive to the child's stage of development

Naturally, our communication with our children needs to be developmentally appropriate. Loading young children with issues and ideas that they cannot understand or that are well beyond their experience may confuse them. Younger children need us to be clear and to keep our sentences concise and uncomplicated. This of course depends on the cognitive level of development of the child.

Some children are bright and very perceptive and may understand more than we expect for their age. When children ask more questions, we continue by giving answers in clear and simple statements. They may stop asking questions and this may be a time to stop giving explanations.

Tuning in to their body language helps us to read how comfortable children are with a particular subject. Probing questions when children do not want to pursue the subject or pressing them for a response will appear intrusive and may result in them not wanting to talk about issues again at a later point in time.

Encourage thinking and problem solving

As parents we often feel that we need to solve our children's problems. However, as our children mature they will need to develop the skills to solve their own problems. Being available to them when they ask questions, rather that trying to probe their minds, goes a long way to developing their sense of self and their ability to think through problems.

By avoiding a tendency to provide all the answers we help our children to work things out for themselves. We make it clear to them that we are there to help if they want to share their thoughts or problems.

We help our children when we give them space to solve their problems and tell them that we believe in them. This enhances their feelings of self worth. If they know that we genuinely believe in them then they develop belief in themselves.

Giving attention and time

We communicate in a positive manner with our children if we give them our full attention when they communicate with us, because we send them the message that what they have to say is important to us. Ignoring or dismissing their comments as immature or silly sends a strong message that we do not value their ideas or thoughts on the subject.

Children need quality time with their parents and carers. Giving time sends them a powerful message that they are important to us and that we regard time with them as worthwhile. Material gifts will never outweigh the importance of the gift of our full attention and time.

As mentioned previously, belief and positive expectation is an essential component of good communication with our children.

Giving love and respect

Love and respect for our child is paramount. Children that do not experience love and appreciation for being the individuals that they are, risk losing faith in themselves and also in others. They are likely to lose respect for themselves and become distrustful of others. The most precious gift we give to our children is our love and respect for them.

Giving them space to think and communicate with others

In a group situation we need to avoid answering questions for our children when they are in conversation with other people. They need the space to think about their responses and to express their own ideas even if they don't have all the appropriate answers. Instead of answering questions for them, they can be gently guided in their interactions with others.

Children are often more perceptive than we realize. We need to give them space to think for themselves, express themselves and allow them to answer their own questions. This pays respect to them, as individuals that have their own thoughts and ideas.

Conclusion

There are many aspects of positive communication with our children and with each other that are worth considering. Giving attention, respect, time and space for communication whilst remaining aware of our own issues and insecurities goes a long way in fostering good communication with our children.

9: Summary of suggestions for nurturing our children

Our hope for our children is that they have a positive self-concept and that they believe in themselves and their abilities, so that they can lead happy and fulfilled lives. The principles have already been mentioned, but they are listed here to summarize the concepts that have been discussed in the book.

1. Understanding the various stages of development

The way in which we help our children will depend on their developmental age because their ability to appreciate and respond to certain concepts will depend on their level of social awareness and their level of understanding of relationships. Therefore as parents we need an understanding of the various stages of child development and how our children are likely to respond and learn at those various stages. This enables us to facilitate their growth and development in a positive manner.

For example, young toddlers may appear self-centred because they do what pleases them and they may seem confident in themselves. They usually explore their environment seemingly unaware of dangers. They need gentle guidance to remain within safe boundaries without over-restricting their desire to learn and explore.

Where they are constantly told 'no' and are constantly restricted when they try or explore something new, they are likely to become anxious and they may withdraw, become agitated or may even become overly active. A gentle balance, between having boundaries and being firm versus giving them freedom to explore, is needed when dealing with their behaviour. The stages of development and the importance of early experiences are discussed in Chapters 1, 2 and 3.

2. Recognizing the importance of rules and boundaries

Children need boundaries and clear rules about expectations for behaviour. They need to learn that there are consequences when they do not comply with the rules. Clear, consistent rules and boundaries need to be taught in the preschool years and are ideally introduced when the child develops motor autonomy, that is, when they start walking and exploring their physical environment.

Young children need space and freedom to explore their environment while being taught safe boundaries within which to explore. Children generally feel more secure where there are clear rules and boundaries regarding their behaviour. Children who learn early what we expect from them are better able to monitor and control their own behaviour. We need to tailor what we expect from our children's behaviour according to their age and stage of development. Chapter 6 deals with rules and boundaries in relation to children's behaviour.

3. Being aware of how we reinforce behaviour

We reinforce our children's behaviour by giving attention to that behaviour. Regardless of whether the behaviour is good or bad it is reinforced when we pay attention to it. Therefore if we want our children to display predominantly good or positive behaviours we need to reinforce these by praise, encouragement and acknowledgement of the good behaviour.

Negative behaviours, if minor, can be ignored but where they are more significant they need to be dealt with by way of consequences and removal of privileges. Issues regarding behaviour management are discussed in Chapter 6.

4. Separate the individual from the behaviour

We are more than our behaviour. We think, then we act and our behaviour is what is evident once we have acted. We can choose to act and therefore behave differently. We need to acknowledge that the individual is a separate entity from their behaviour. Understanding this psychological fact enables us to avoid making our children feel worthless when they have done something wrong in their behaviour towards us or towards others.

By telling our children that they are bad and that we disapprove of them erodes their self-esteem. However, we can tell them that their behaviour is bad and that we are disappointed in their behaviour, and that we expect better behaviour from them as individuals. Then we are making it clear that they are not synonymous with their behaviour. They can choose to act differently and more appropriately next time. This process protects their self-esteem. It allows us to discipline the unacceptable behaviour while remaining positive and encouraging towards the individual.

5. Learning about responsibility

As growing individuals our children need to learn to take responsibility for their behaviour. The important issue of personal responsibility is discussed in Chapter 7. We should not make excuses for them when they misbehave. Children need to learn to apologize to those whom they have hurt in any way. They need to learn that there are both negative and positive consequences to their behaviour.

When children learn to take responsibility for their behaviour and are taught to apologize to those whom they have wronged they become sensitive adults who care about the well-being of others. And in this way children are encouraged to learn from their mistakes and behave more appropriately next time.

6. Our children learn from our example

We help our children when we remain aware of our own behaviour and recognise that our children model their behaviour on ours. If we engage in inappropriate behaviours then our children are likely to engage in similar behaviours.

If we do not treat our children with respect then we cannot expect them to show respect towards us. If we deal aggressively with others then we must not be surprised if our children behave in an aggressive manner towards us or towards others.

Where we show thoughtfulness and kindness towards others we raise children that are thoughtful, kind and caring. Where we show care for our environment and respect for other living creatures we raise children that develop similar qualities.

7. Remaining aware of how we communicate with our children

The words that we use in communication with others have a powerful effect on them. If we use negative language or use words that show we have doubt about our children's abilities or future then we hinder their ability to develop belief in themselves. We need continually to tap into the positive inner self in our children to allow their self-concept to flourish and grow.

We reinforce self-confidence and a positive self-concept in our children when we tell and show them that we believe in them and in their abilities. Tuning in to their particular strengths enables us to nurture their self-confidence in their abilities. By respecting them and their ideas we send them a powerful message that they are worthy individuals and that their ideas are noted and are important to us. Even if they are mistaken or make errors we can acknowledge their efforts as they grow and learn.

When we hold feelings of fear or anxiety about our children they pick up on the non-verbal cues that we subtly send them and they begin to doubt themselves. The best gift we can give our children is to love and have faith in them.

Remaining positive in communication with our children is particularly difficult when their behaviour is uncooperative and non-compliant. At this time it is important that we remain firm about behavioural expectations and that we use appropriate discipline techniques to curb the behaviour, while remaining positive towards the individual. Chapter 8 outlines important issues about communication.

8. Being available to provide guidance and support

Our children need our guidance when it comes to exploring their world. We instill values in our children based on our own beliefs. Children will need guidance especially where their behaviour is inappropriate or unacceptable. This is where the importance of rules and boundaries for behaviour again becomes evident.

When we give support we need to avoid the tendency to criticize our children for their choices and decisions. Instead we can try to understand why they have made those choices. Then we will be able to give more appropriate guidance as they move along their particular path in life. Guidance given with love, respect and support is of greater value and goes much further than guidance given with judgement and criticism.

9. Examining our own attitudes and beliefs

Our beliefs influence the way we think, feel and act. Therefore our beliefs influence our behaviour and at the same time it influences how we interact with others and with our children. Our children pick up on our beliefs and these beliefs have an influence on their lives as well.

If as adults we have a clear understanding of our own beliefs and why we hold on to them, we can give our children a clearer understanding of our values and belief system. If we are unsure of our own beliefs and motives for our behaviour then our children, as well as others, will be more likely to challenge our belief system and pick holes in it.

'Know thyself' is a wise proverb. Unless we know ourselves we cannot impart a real sense of values to our children.

10. Respecting the individuality of our children

Respecting the individuality of our children allows them to develop their unique sense of purpose and meaning for their lives. We nurture self-respect and confidence in them when we treat them with love and respect. Our children are developing human beings and they deserve to be respected.

Our children do not exist to boost our confidence, our self worth or our self-esteem as parents. They exist in their own right and we are privileged to be able to guide them along their way.

We show lack of respect for our children when we do not value their opinions and ideas about their own experiences. Listening to our children and to what they have to say allows them to feel that they are respected for who they are as individuals. Listening to them also validates their feelings, so that they learn that their feelings are important to us. They are then more likely to remain in touch with their feelings as they develop into adulthood.

Respect for our children also involves believing in them and their unique abilities. Once we have provided them with guidance and teaching in their formative years, we need to have faith that they will find their own paths and live their own lives in healthy and positive ways.

11. Whether young or older, our children need our time and our involvement

Spending time with our children gives them a powerful message that they are worthy and that we consider spending time with them as important. When we do creative and fun activities with our children it not only benefits them but it benefits us as well for many different reasons. It reminds us of the joyful times that we had as children. The shared activities invariably result in laughter, fun and even adventure, and these experiences are beneficial to our health and well-being.

Spending time with our children also allows us to understand how they think so that we can know what is important to them. It allows communication with our children to develop and remain open. It should come as no surprise to us if our children do not communicate with us when they grow older, if we had no time for them when they were younger.

Spending time with our children also enables us to continue to guide and teach them on a daily basis, even in little ways, from an early age and as they grow into young adults. While preschool is a precious time for teaching children about rules, boundaries and responsibility, the importance of ongoing guidance through their middle childhood years and adolescence should not be underestimated. One developmental stage is no more important than the other.

We need to remain aware that our children need our love, support and involvement in their lives throughout childhood and even when they reach the independence of adulthood.

12. Recognizing the importance of failure and learning from our mistakes

Accepting failure as part of our development in all aspects of our lives enables us to empower our children when they make mistakes. They learn from our example that they do not dissolve or die if they make a mistake. Instead they learn that by making mistakes we all learn and find better ways of doing things. They also learn that failure is part of the process of achieving our goals.

This means that as adults we need to tolerate mistakes that we, or others, make as part of the process of life. No one is perfect. We all make errors. Children who tend to be perfectionists especially need to learn that mistakes will occur and that it is part of life. Mistakes allow them to learn important lessons about being more tolerant when others make mistakes too.

The expectation that everything must be perfect sets us up for disappointment and regret when our unrealistically high standards are not met. Learning to live 'with the flow' enables us to take the good with the bad and learn from all our experiences. Our children learn these lessons from us by observing our reactions to disappointment.

13. Avoiding being over focused on themselves

Children learn with time that they are part of the greater community of mankind. In time they come to choose their particular path and find their individual purpose in life. We help our children when we encourage them to avoid being over focused on their needs and their own particular issues. They could be encouraged to learn about the lives of others less fortunate than themselves. Thus they may learn help others in some small way.

When our children are over focused on themselves, their physical desires and material possessions, they become overly self-conscious and are inclined to continually compare themselves to others. In this way they will never be satisfied, because there will always be others who have more material goods, better physical appearance or greater status than themselves. By thinking in this way they run the risk of feeling that they are never good enough and they may become unhappy or even depressed.

Learning to love themselves and to remain true to their own talents and abilities allows our children to see that they have a special and unique place in the universe. This knowledge enables them to see that they can uniquely help others in a way that no one else can.

By encouraging our children to spread joy and love to others, even in little ways, they learn that they can have a positive effect on another's life. Their positive act towards one individual can, in turn, lead to that individual behaving more positively and lovingly towards another, and consequently the power of love is magnified and spreads further than they could ever imagine. This is possibly their most important lesson.

14. Remember to have FUN with our children.

Whilst there may appear to be many dos and don'ts when reading about your child's development we need to remember, above all, to have fun with our children. We all learn more effectively in an atmosphere of fun and enjoyment, and in the same way our children learn more when they are happy and when they enjoy being with their parents.

We also need to maintain our sense of humour. No matter how difficult issues or situations may seem, there will always be something to be grateful for and to feel positive about. So we should aim to enjoy time with our children as we learn more about life together.

15. Finally

Our children are the future. As parents we have the privilege of being involved in their lives. We can be confident that with our love and respect our children will develop into happy and secure individuals who will have a positive influence on the lives of others in their future.

Index

A

acceptance, 24
achievements, 26
adolescent, 11, 36
adulthood, 47, 60
aggression, 6, 39
anxiety, 1
apology, 17
approval, 38, 47
attention, 38, 51
attitudes, 10
authority, 10
autonomy, 4, 35

B

behaviour, 4, 35, 37, 57, 58
behaviours escalating, 38
belief, 29, 32
beliefs, 11, 27, 50, 59
bonding, 2, 3, 15
boundaries, 13, 35, 56
bullying, 46

C

cognitive, 50
cognitive development, 3, 18
communication, 5, 13, 14, 43, 49, 50, 53, 58
community, 24, 62
confidence, 49
consequences, 36, 37, 39, 45
consistency, 13
consistent, 36
contract, 37
control, 40, 41
counselling, 47
creativity, 37

D

development, 9, 10, 43, 50, 55
developmentally delayed, 5
discipline, 40, 41, 43, 57

E

enjoyment, 63
enlightened, 10
environment, 1, 23, 24, 49
example, 12
excuses, 45
expectation, 52, 62
expectations, 25
experience, 22, 25, 34
experiences, 1, 56, 62
experimenting, 11
exploration, 5, 36
extended family, 2, 15

F

failure, 62
faith, 33
fear, 39
fearfulness, 5
fears, 50
frustrated, 39
frustration, 40

G

growth, 4
guidance, 29, 31, 33, 41, 42, 59, 61

Lightning Source UK Ltd.
Milton Keynes UK
UKOW04f0818231217
314970UK00001B/54/P